Frederick Douglass

Barbara Kramer

NATIONAL
GEOGRAPHIC

Washington, D.C.

To my writers' group—Karry, Barb, and Barb —B. K.

Published by National Geographic Partners, LLC, Washington, D.C. 20036.

Library of Congress Cataloging-in-Publication Data

Names: Kramer, Barbara, author.
Title: Frederick Douglass / Barbara Kramer.
Description: Washington, DC : National Geographic, 2017. | Series: National
  Geographic readers
Identifiers: LCCN 2016038837 (print) | LCCN 2016040010 (ebook) | ISBN
  9781426327568 (pbk. : alk. paper) | ISBN 9781426327575 (hardcover : alk.
  paper) | ISBN 9781426327582 (e-book)
Subjects: LCSH: Douglass, Frederick, 1818-1895—Juvenile literature. |
  African American abolitionists—Biography—Juvenile literature. |
  Slaves—United States—Biography—Juvenile literature. | Slavery—United
  States—History—Juvenile literature.
Classification: LCC E449.D75 K73 2017 (print) | LCC E449.D75 (ebook) | DDC
  973.8092 [B] —dc23

LC record available at lccn.loc.gov/2016038837

The publisher and author gratefully acknowledge the expert content review of this book by Robert S. Levine, Ph.D., Department of English, University of Maryland, and author of several titles on Frederick Douglass, including *The Lives of Frederick Douglass* (2015), and the literacy review of this book by Mariam Jean Dreher, professor of reading education, University of Maryland, College Park.

National Geographic supports K–12 educators with ELA Common Core Resources. Visit natgeoed.org/commoncore for more information.

Printed in the United States of America
16/WOR/1

Table of Contents

Who Was Frederick Douglass?

a painting of
Frederick Douglass,
from around 1844

Frederick Douglass was born a slave. He worked hard for his master for no money. His master told Douglass where to live, what to eat, and what to do.

After 20 years as a slave, Douglass escaped. He began speaking out against slavery. He didn't stop until all slaves were free. Then he worked to help freed slaves have better lives.

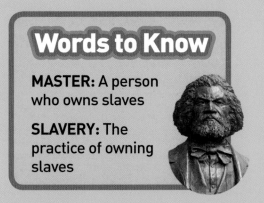

Words to Know

MASTER: A person who owns slaves

SLAVERY: The practice of owning slaves

Born a Slave

Douglass was born in February 1818 on a farm in Talbot County, Maryland, U.S.A. Soon after his birth, his mother was sent to work on another farm. Douglass only saw her four or five times. She died when he was seven. He never knew his father.

a wood engraving of slaves working with cotton in the American South

As an adult, Douglass had this cabin built in his backyard in Washington, D.C. It looked like the one where he had lived with his grandparents.

Douglass spent his early years with his grandparents. They lived in a cabin about 12 miles from his master's farm.

When Douglass was about six years old, his grandmother took him to their master's farm. She didn't want to leave him there, but she had to do what their owner said. Douglass knew then that he was expected to obey the master, too.

About two years later, Douglass was sent to Baltimore, Maryland, to work. He had heard stories about that city and was excited to go.

In His Own Words

"I didn't know I was a slave until I found out I couldn't do the things I wanted."

Baltimore Harbor in 1831, during the time Douglass lived there

In His Time

In the 1820s, growing up as a slave was very different from growing up as a child who was free.

SCHOOL: Slaves did not attend school. Teaching a slave to read was against the law in some states. An education would give a slave power.

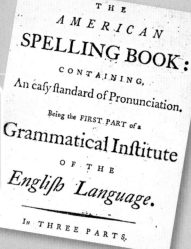

THE
AMERICAN
SPELLING BOOK:
CONTAINING,
An eafy ftandard of Pronunciation.
Being the FIRST PART of a
Grammatical Inftitute
OF THE
Englifh Language.

IN THREE PARTS.

EVENTS: Some people helped slaves escape from their masters. The group of people who led slaves to safety was called the Underground Railroad.

Please to let Benjamin McDaniel pass to Dr. Henkal's in New-Market, Shenandoah County, Va. or Tuesday next Montpellier, for Mrs. Madison and return on Monday.

June 1st 1843.

TRAVEL: Slaves who traveled without their owners had to carry a pass from their masters. Black people who were free had to carry papers saying they were not slaves.

RIGHTS: Slaves had no rights. Slaves were listed as property along with the slave owner's animals. They could be sold to other slave owners at any time, often separating children from their parents.

FREEDOM: When their masters died, a few slaves were given their freedom. But most got new owners, so they were still not free. Sometimes slaves could buy their freedom. But since most slaves did not earn money for their work, that rarely happened.

Words to Know

FREEDOM: The power to move or act as you wish and do what you want to do

Learning to Read

In Baltimore, Douglass worked
for Hugh Auld (HUE ALLD)
and his wife. He took care of
their young son and ran errands.
Mrs. Auld started teaching Douglass
to read. Mr. Auld told her to stop.
He said slaves should know only one
thing—how to obey their master.

But Douglass kept learning. He gave
biscuits (BISS-kits) to poor white
children he met on his errands.
In return, they helped him read.

This wood engraving shows Mrs. Auld teaching Douglass to read.

That's a FACT! With 50 cents Douglass earned from polishing shoes, he bought a book of famous speeches and read it many times.

13

When Douglass was 15, he was sent back to the farm. His master had died. He now had a new owner. Douglass had to work hard in the field. He was often treated badly. He tried to escape, but he was caught.

Slaves often worked long hours in the fields. They worked on a large farm or group of farms called a plantation.

Other slave owners were angry. Douglass had set a bad example for their slaves. To avoid trouble, Douglass's new master sent Douglass back to Baltimore to work for the Auld family again.

That's a **FACT!** When Douglass was working as a field slave, he held secret classes to teach other slaves to read.

Runaway Slave

In Baltimore, Douglass met free black people. He fell in love with a free black woman named Anna Murray. More than ever, he wanted to be free.

On September 3, 1838, he tried to escape again. He headed north by boat and train. If he were caught, he might be killed or sold. But he made it to New York, a free state. He sent for Anna, and they got married.

Words to Know

FREE STATE: A U.S. state that did not allow people to own slaves

That's a FACT! Over time, Douglass and Anna had five children: three boys and two girls.

an illustration of Douglass and his wife, Anna, soon after they were married

an artist's view of New Bedford, Massachusetts, around the time Douglass was there

Douglass and Anna moved to New Bedford, Massachusetts, U.S.A. There Douglass met people who wanted to abolish (uh–BALL–ish) slavery.

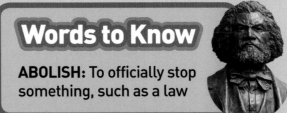

Words to Know

ABOLISH: To officially stop something, such as a law

In 1841, he spoke at one of their meetings. Douglass told the crowd about his life as a slave. The people liked his speech. Douglass soon began traveling to many states giving speeches about slavery. He also wrote a book about his life as a slave.

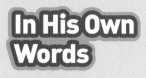

In His Own Words

"I longed to have a future—a future with hope in it."

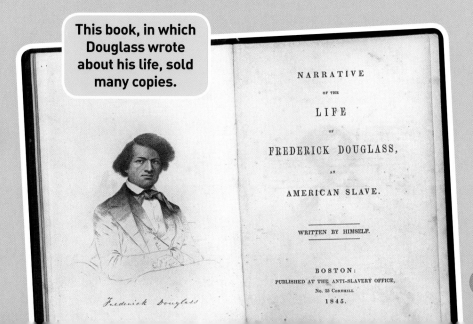

This book, in which Douglass wrote about his life, sold many copies.

NARRATIVE

OF THE

LIFE

OF

FREDERICK DOUGLASS,

AN

AMERICAN SLAVE.

WRITTEN BY HIMSELF.

BOSTON:
PUBLISHED AT THE ANTI-SLAVERY OFFICE,
No. 25 CORNHILL
1845.

Frederick Douglass

19

Douglass had escaped, but he was still a slave. Soon he became well known for his speeches and his book. That put him in danger. Now it was easier for his master to find him. Douglass had to get away. But it meant leaving his family behind.

Many people wanted to hear Douglass speak. He talked about the abolition of slavery, which is the act of ending slavery.

an illustration of a steamship similar to the one on which Douglass traveled to England

He sailed to England. He gave speeches there and made many friends. They raised money to buy his freedom. At last, Douglass was free!

6 COOL FACTS About Douglass

1 As a young man in Baltimore, Douglass learned to play the violin. It was a hobby he enjoyed the rest of his life.

2 Douglass met with President Abraham Lincoln three times during the Civil War. After the president died, Mrs. Lincoln gave her husband's favorite walking stick to Douglass.

3 Douglass became active in the Underground Railroad. His home in Rochester, New York, was a stopping place. Runaway slaves could hide there until it was safe to travel to the next stop. Today, people can visit there.

4 Douglass was known as a great storyteller. He often made family, friends, and audiences laugh with his tales.

Douglass wrote three books about his life: *Narrative of the Life of Frederick Douglass, My Bondage and My Freedom,* and *Life and Times of Frederick Douglass.*

5

EIGHTEENTH THOUSAND.

MY BONDAGE
AND
MY FREEDOM.

Part I.—Life as a Slave. Part II.—Life as a Freeman.

BY FREDERICK DOUGLASS.
WITH
AN INTRODUCTION.
BY DR. JAMES McCUNE SMITH.

NEW YORK AND AUBURN:
MILLER, ORTON & CO.
1857.

6 In 1899, four years after Douglass died, a statue of him was built in Rochester, New York. It was the first time an African American was honored with a statue.

A Fight to End Slavery

In 1847, Douglass returned to the United States. He moved his family to Rochester, New York. There he started a newspaper called the *North Star*. He wrote articles against slavery for the paper.

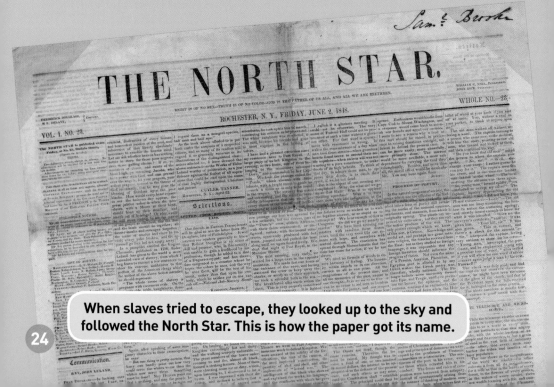

When slaves tried to escape, they looked up to the sky and followed the North Star. This is how the paper got its name.

Charles Douglass

Lewis Douglass

Two of Douglass's sons were among the first African Americans to sign up to fight in the Civil War.

People in the United States did not agree about slavery. That led to the start of the Civil War in 1861. Douglass organized a group of African Americans to fight in that war.

Words to Know

CIVIL WAR: A war between different groups of people from the same country

New Beginnings

The Civil War led to the end of slavery. But black people were still not treated the same as white people. Douglass gave speeches about treating all people the same.

In His Own Words

"I would unite with anybody to do right and with nobody to do wrong."

1818
Born in February

1824
Sent to live on his master's farm

1826
Begins work as a house slave in Baltimore

Douglass with Helen Pitts

In 1882, Anna got sick and died. Douglass was sad and lonely. About two years later, he married Helen Pitts. That upset many people because Helen was white.

1838
Escapes from slavery; marries Anna Murray

1841
Gives his first speech against slavery

Douglass never stopped speaking out to help others. On February 20, 1895, he gave a speech to a women's group. He died at home later that day. He was 77 years old.

Douglass at work in the library at Cedar Hill, his home in Washington, D.C.

1845
Publishes the first of three books about his life

1846
Friends in England buy his freedom

"Abolition of slavery had been the deepest desire and the great labor of my life."

Douglass was a powerful voice for those who believe that all people should be treated equally. Today, his words still inspire others all over the world.

a statue of Douglass in the United States Capitol Building in Washington, D.C.

1847
Starts his newspaper, the *North Star*

1884
Marries Helen Pitts

1895
Dies on February 20

QUIZ WHIZ

See how many questions you can get right!
Answers are at the bottom of page 31.

1

Who took care of Douglass until he was about six years old?

A. his master's wife
B. his mother
C. his aunt
D. his grandmother

Net Ox
Owl Hen
Pan Bee

2

The first person to help Douglass learn to read was _____.

A. a white friend
B. his grandmother
C. Mrs. Auld
D. another slave

How old was Douglass when he was sent back to the farm after living in Baltimore?

A. 12
B. 15
C. 18
D. 20

3

Douglas was still a slave when he escaped Baltimore to go to New York.

A. true
B. false

Douglass traveled to what country to keep from being caught and returned to his master?

A. Senegal
B. Canada
C. England
D. Mexico

Douglass started a newspaper called _____.

A. the *Underground Railroad*
B. the *North Star*
C. the *Slave Papers*
D. the *Life and Times of Frederick Douglass*

Which one of these statements about slavery is true?

A. Slaves could travel where they wanted.
B. Young slaves were taught to read.
C. Slaves who escaped to free states were safe.
D. Slaves had to obey their masters.

ABOLISH: To officially stop something, such as a law

CIVIL WAR: A war between different groups of people from the same country

FREE STATE: A U.S. state that did not allow people to own slaves

FREEDOM: The power to move or act as you wish and do what you want to do

MASTER: A person who owns slaves

SLAVERY: The practice of owning slaves